HAL•LEONARD
INSTRUMENTAL
PLAY-ALONG

AUDIO ACCESS INCLUDED

CELLO

Piazzolla Tangos

To access audio visit:
www.halleonard.com/mylibrary

Enter Code
4090-6125-0572-2019

ISBN 978-1-4950-2845-8

BOOSEY&HAWKES

AN IMAGEM COMPANY

DISTRIBUTED BY

HAL•LEONARD®
CORPORATION
7777 W. BLUEMOUND RD. P.O. BOX 13819 MILWAUKEE, WI 53213

www.boosey.com
www.halleonard.com

AUSENCIAS
(The Absent)

CELLO

ASTOR PIAZZOLLA

EL VIAJE
(The Voyage)

CELLO

ASTOR PIAZZOLLA

CHANSON DE LA NAISSANCE
(Song of the Birth)
from FAMILLE D'ARTISTES

CELLO

ASTOR PIAZZOLLA

MILONGA
from A MIDSUMMER NIGHT'S DREAM

CELLO

ASTOR PIAZZOLLA

LIBERTANGO

CELLO

ASTOR PIAZZOLLA

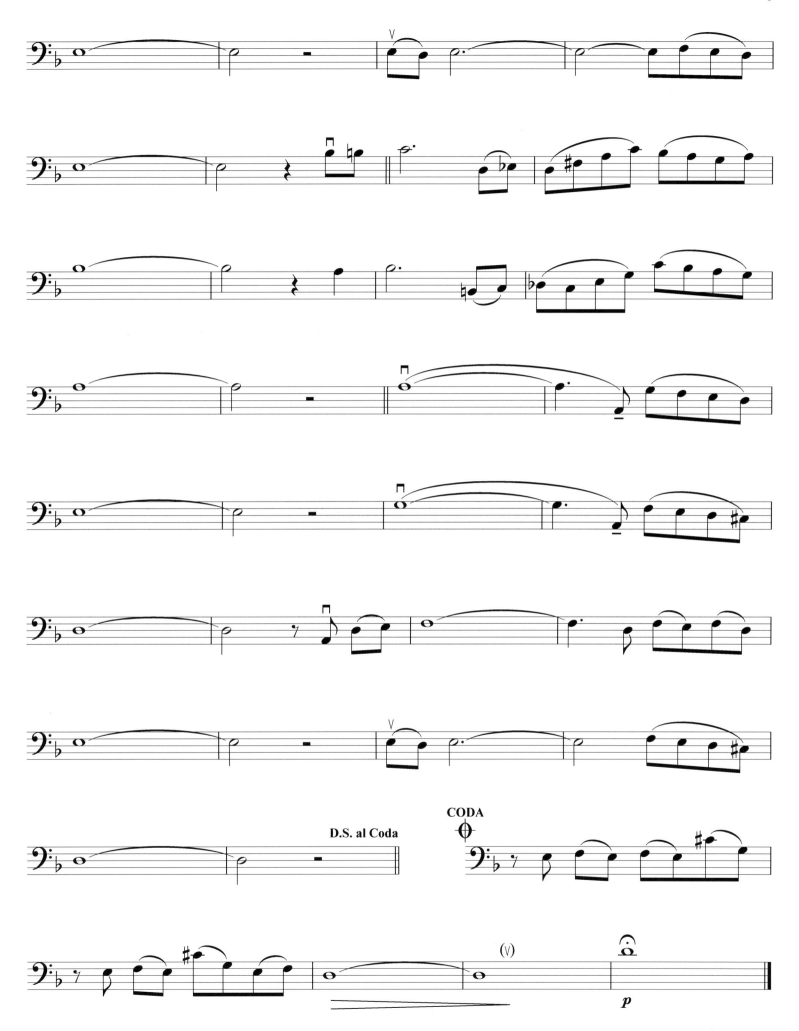

LOS SUEÑOS
(Dreams)
from SUR

CELLO

ASTOR PIAZZOLLA

OBLIVION

CELLO

ASTOR PIAZZOLLA

OUVERTURE
from FAMILLE D'ARTISTES

CELLO

ASTOR PIAZZOLLA

SENSUEL
(Sensual)
from A MIDSUMMER NIGHT'S DREAM

CELLO

ASTOR PIAZZOLLA

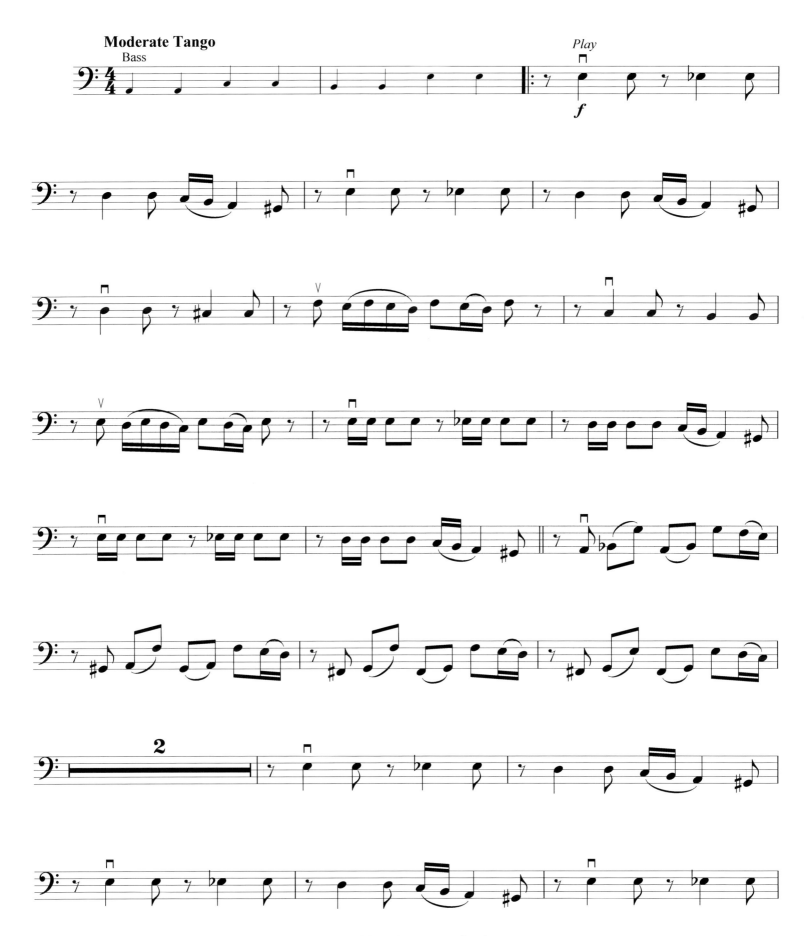

SENTIMENTAL
from FAMILLE D'ARTISTES

ASTOR PIAZZOLLA

CELLO

VUELVO AL SUR
(I'm Returning South)

CELLO

ASTOR PIAZZOLLA

SIN RUMBO
(Aimless)

CELLO

ASTOR PIAZZOLLA

STREET TANGO

CELLO

ASTOR PIAZZOLLA

TANGO FINAL
from FAMILLE D'ARTISTES

CELLO

ASTOR PIAZZOLLA

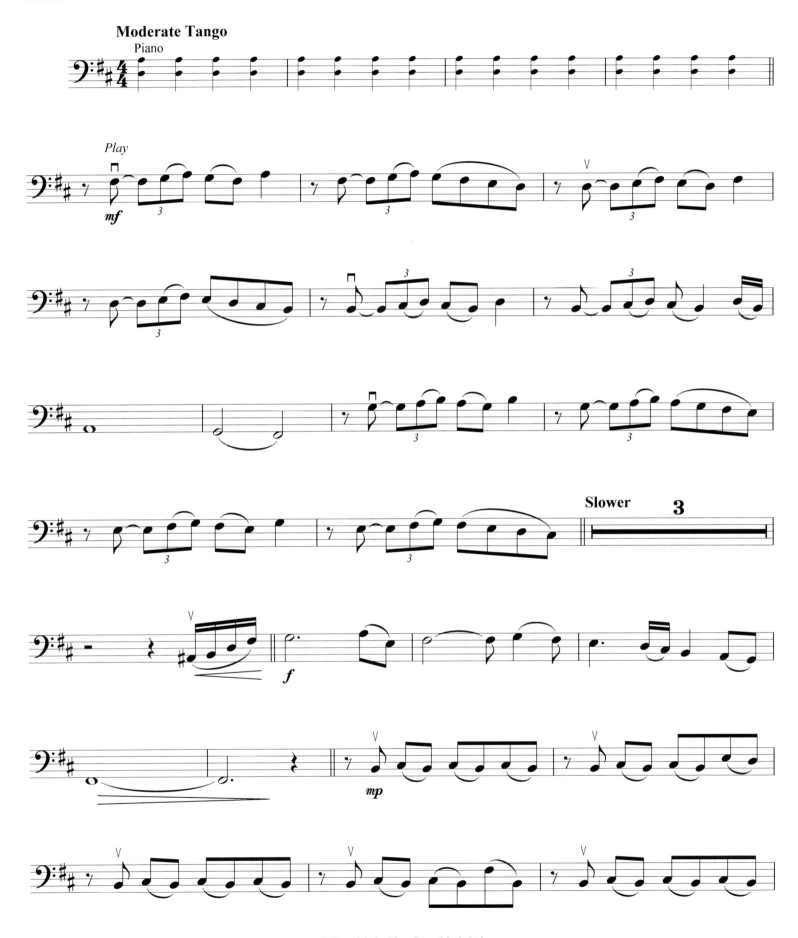